The Moon Landing

American history, Volume 12

Michael Johnson

Published by Harmony House Publishing, 2024.

THE MOON LANDING

First edition. April 5, 2024.

ISBN: 979-8224403202

Written by Michael Johnson.

Table of Contents

"To the dreamers, the explorers, and the believers in the power of human ingenuity,This book is dedicated to all those who dared to reach for the stars, fueled by curiosity and driven by a relentless pursuit of knowledge. To the astronauts who risked everything to push the boundaries of what was possible, and to the countless scientists, engineers, and visionaries who worked tirelessly behind the scenes to make the impossible a reality.May the story of the moon landing inspire future generations to continue pushing the boundaries of exploration and discovery, and may it serve as a reminder of the boundless potential that lies within each of us.This book is dedicated to the dreamers who dare to reach for the stars.With gratitude and admiration,Michael Johnson"

Chapter 1: Introduction

The 20th century saw the dawn of a new era in human history: the Space Age. It was a time of unprecedented scientific achievement and geopolitical tension as the United States and the Soviet Union engaged in a fierce competition known as the Space Race. At the heart of this rivalry lay the audacious goal of landing a man on the moon—a goal that would come to symbolize humanity's boundless ambition and capacity for exploration.

The roots of the Space Race can be traced back to the aftermath of World War II. As the Cold War escalated between the United States and the Soviet Union, so too did their rivalry in the realm of space exploration. Both superpowers recognized the potential strategic and ideological significance of conquering the cosmos, and thus began a race to achieve milestones in space technology and exploration.

In the late 1950s, the Soviet Union stunned the world with the launch of Sputnik 1, the first artificial satellite, in October 1957. This momentous event marked the beginning of the Space Age and signaled the Soviet Union's technological prowess to the world. The successful launch of Sputnik not only demonstrated Soviet superiority in space technology but also raised concerns among Americans about their own scientific and military capabilities.

The launch of Sputnik ignited a sense of urgency in the United States to catch up and surpass the Soviet Union in the field of space exploration. In response, President Dwight D. Eisenhower established the National Aeronautics and Space Administration (NASA) in 1958, with the mandate to lead American efforts in space exploration and research. NASA quickly became the focal point of America's ambitions to assert its dominance in space and demonstrate the superiority of the democratic capitalist system over communism.

The cultural and political climate of the time played a crucial role in shaping America's determination to land a man on the moon. The

1960s were a decade of profound social and political upheaval in the United States, marked by the civil rights movement, the Vietnam War, and the countercultural revolution. Against this backdrop of turmoil and uncertainty, the space program emerged as a source of national pride and unity—a symbol of American ingenuity and determination in the face of adversity.

Key political figures such as President John F. Kennedy played a pivotal role in galvanizing public support for the moon landing mission. In a speech to Congress on May 25, 1961, President Kennedy set forth the ambitious goal of landing a man on the moon and returning him safely to Earth before the end of the decade. This bold declaration captured the imagination of the American people and rallied support behind the space program.

The Apollo program, NASA's flagship initiative aimed at achieving President Kennedy's lunar landing goal, involved a vast network of scientists, engineers, and astronauts working tirelessly to overcome the immense technical challenges of space travel. At its core, the Apollo program represented a triumph of human ingenuity and collaboration, as thousands of individuals across the United States came together to achieve a common goal.

Key players in the Apollo program included legendary figures such as Dr. Wernher von Braun, the German-born rocket engineer who played a central role in the development of the Saturn V rocket—the most powerful rocket ever built. Von Braun's visionary leadership and technical expertise were instrumental in making the moon landing a reality.

Another key figure in the Apollo program was astronaut Neil Armstrong, who would ultimately become the first human to set foot on the lunar surface. Armstrong, along with fellow astronauts Buzz Aldrin and Michael Collins, embarked on the historic Apollo 11 mission in July 1969, carrying the hopes and dreams of an entire nation with them.

Throughout the 1960s, NASA worked tirelessly to overcome the numerous technical, logistical, and safety challenges posed by the lunar landing mission. From developing the spacecraft and launch vehicles to training astronauts and conducting rigorous testing and simulations, every aspect of the Apollo program was meticulously planned and executed with the utmost precision.

As the world watched with bated breath, the Apollo 11 mission culminated in one of the most iconic moments in human history: Neil Armstrong's immortal words as he set foot on the lunar surface—"That's one small step for man, one giant leap for mankind." With these words, Armstrong captured the essence of humanity's quest for exploration and discovery, and forever cemented the moon landing as a defining moment in the annals of history.

In the chapters that follow, we will delve deeper into the epic saga of the Apollo program, from its humble beginnings to its triumphant conclusion. We will explore the technological marvels and human dramas that unfolded along the way, and reflect on the enduring legacy of America's giant leap for mankind.

Chapter 2: The Space Race Begins

The Space Race of the 20th century ignited a fervent competition between two global superpowers—the United States and the Soviet Union. It was a race fueled by political ideology, national pride, and technological prowess, as both nations sought to assert their dominance in the realm of space exploration. This chapter delves into the early achievements and milestones that set the stage for the Space Race, examining the launch of Sputnik by the Soviet Union and its profound impact on American perceptions of technological superiority. It also explores the formation of NASA and its ambitious mission to put a man on the moon.

Exploring Early Achievements in Space Exploration:

The dawn of the Space Age can be traced back to the aftermath of World War II, as former adversaries turned their attention to the stars in a quest for scientific and strategic supremacy. In the years following the war, both the United States and the Soviet Union made significant strides in rocket technology and space exploration, laying the groundwork for the Space Race that would define much of the Cold War era.

One of the earliest milestones in space exploration came in 1944, when German scientist Wernher von Braun successfully launched the V-2 rocket—the world's first long-range guided ballistic missile. Developed by Nazi Germany during World War II, the V-2 rocket laid the foundation for future advancements in rocketry and space exploration, serving as a precursor to the rockets that would eventually carry humans into space.

Following the end of World War II, the United States and the Soviet Union engaged in a race to acquire German rocket technology and expertise, with both nations recognizing the potential military and strategic benefits of rocketry. In the United States, the capture of German scientists and engineers, including Wernher von Braun, paved the way for the development of the country's own rocket program under the auspices of the newly formed Army Ballistic Missile Agency.

Meanwhile, in the Soviet Union, scientists and engineers led by Sergei Korolev were making rapid advances in rocket technology, culminating in the successful launch of the R-7 rocket in 1957. This powerful intercontinental ballistic missile, capable of delivering nuclear warheads to targets thousands of kilometers away, would later serve as the basis for the Soviet space program's early achievements.

The Launch of Sputnik and Its Impact:

On October 4, 1957, the Soviet Union achieved a historic milestone in space exploration with the launch of Sputnik 1—the world's first artificial satellite. Weighing just 184 pounds (83.6 kilograms), Sputnik 1 was a spherical metal orb equipped with four external radio antennas that broadcasted a simple radio signal back to Earth.

The launch of Sputnik sent shockwaves across the globe and sparked a wave of anxiety and uncertainty in the United States. For many Americans, the sight of a Soviet satellite orbiting overhead served as a sobering reminder of the technological prowess of their Cold War rival—and raised troubling questions about America's own scientific and military capabilities.

In the aftermath of the Sputnik launch, American perceptions of technological superiority were shaken to their core. The notion of American exceptionalism, which had long been a cornerstone of national identity, was called into question as the Soviet Union demonstrated its ability to achieve a significant technological feat before the eyes of the world.

The formation of NASA and Its Mission to Land

a Man on the Moon:

Amid growing concerns about America's lagging space program, President Dwight D. Eisenhower took decisive action to address the nation's shortcomings in space exploration. On July 29, 1958, President Eisenhower signed into law the National Aeronautics and Space Act, which established the National Aeronautics and Space Administration (NASA) as the primary agency responsible for coordinating America's civilian space activities.

NASA was tasked with a bold and ambitious mission: to lead the United States in space exploration, scientific research, and technological innovation. From its inception, NASA embodied the spirit of American ingenuity and determination, marshaling the resources and talent necessary to propel the nation into the forefront of space exploration.

Central to NASA's mission was the goal of landing a man on the moon—a goal that would come to define the agency's efforts in the years to come. In 1961, President John F. Kennedy made history when he declared before a joint session of Congress the ambitious challenge of landing a man on the moon and returning him safely to Earth before the end of the decade.

Kennedy's bold proclamation set the stage for one of the most audacious endeavors in human history—the Apollo program. Under the leadership of NASA Administrator James E. Webb, the Apollo program brought together the brightest minds in science, engineering, and astronautics to tackle the monumental challenges of lunar exploration.

From the development of the Saturn V rocket—the most powerful rocket ever built—to the rigorous training of astronauts and the meticulous planning of lunar missions, every aspect of the Apollo program was geared towards achieving the goal set forth by President Kennedy. It was a mission that captured the imagination of the American people and inspired a generation to reach for the stars.

As the United States embarked on its journey to the moon, the stage was set for an epic showdown between two global superpowers. The

Space Race had begun in earnest, and the world watched with bated breath as America and the Soviet Union vied for supremacy in the final frontier.

Chapter 3: Project Apollo

Project Apollo stands as one of humanity's greatest achievements, representing the culmination of years of research, innovation, and perseverance in the quest to reach the moon. This chapter delves into the development of the Apollo spacecraft, the formidable challenges faced by engineers and scientists, the tragic loss of the Apollo 1 astronauts, and the subsequent safety improvements that transformed the program. Despite setbacks and obstacles, the determination of the Apollo program never wavered, ultimately leading to one of the most iconic moments in human history—the successful landing of astronauts on the lunar surface.

Development of the Apollo Spacecraft:

The genesis of the Apollo program can be traced back to the early years of NASA, when the agency embarked on an ambitious quest to fulfill President John F. Kennedy's vision of landing a man on the moon before the end of the 1960s. Central to this mission was the development of the Apollo spacecraft—a complex and innovative spacecraft designed to transport astronauts to the moon and back safely.

The Apollo spacecraft consisted of multiple components, each meticulously engineered to withstand the rigors of space travel and lunar landing. At its core was the Command Module (CM), which served as the primary living quarters and control center for the crew during their journey to the moon and back. The CM was equipped with essential systems for navigation, communication, and life support, ensuring the safety and well-being of the astronauts throughout their mission.

Accompanying the CM was the Lunar Module (LM), a specialized spacecraft designed to transport astronauts from lunar orbit to the surface of the moon and back. The LM featured a descent stage for landing on the lunar surface and an ascent stage for returning to lunar orbit, making it a crucial component of the Apollo lunar landing missions.

The development of the Apollo spacecraft presented a host of technical and engineering challenges for NASA and its contractors. From designing lightweight yet durable materials to developing advanced propulsion systems and life support technologies, every aspect of the spacecraft had to be carefully crafted and tested to withstand the harsh conditions of space travel.

One of the most significant engineering feats of the Apollo program was the development of the Saturn V rocket—the largest and most powerful rocket ever built. Standing over 363 feet tall and capable of generating over 7.5 million pounds of thrust, the Saturn V was instrumental in propelling the Apollo spacecraft on their journey to the moon.

Throughout the 1960s, NASA and its contractors worked tirelessly to overcome the myriad technical challenges of the Apollo program. From the heat-resistant materials used in the spacecraft's reentry shields to the precision engineering of its guidance and navigation systems, every aspect of the Apollo spacecraft was subjected to rigorous testing and evaluation to ensure its reliability and safety.

Tragic Loss of Apollo 1 and Subsequent Safety Improvements:

Despite the meticulous planning and rigorous testing that went into the Apollo program, tragedy struck on January 27, 1967, during a preflight test for the Apollo 1 mission. A fire broke out in the command module of the spacecraft, claiming the lives of astronauts Gus Grissom, Ed White, and Roger Chaffee.

The loss of the Apollo 1 crew sent shockwaves through NASA and the nation, prompting a comprehensive review of the Apollo program's safety protocols and procedures. Investigators identified numerous design flaws and safety deficiencies that contributed to the tragedy, including the spacecraft's highly flammable cabin atmosphere and inadequate fire suppression systems.

In the wake of the Apollo 1 disaster, NASA implemented sweeping changes to improve the safety and reliability of the Apollo spacecraft. These included redesigning the command module to eliminate flammable materials, improving ventilation and fire detection systems, and enhancing crew escape mechanisms in the event of an emergency.

NASA also instituted stricter testing and inspection protocols to ensure the integrity of the spacecraft and its systems. Every component of the Apollo spacecraft was subjected to rigorous testing and analysis to identify potential failure points and mitigate risks before flight.

The determination of the Apollo program:

Despite the setbacks and challenges posed by the Apollo 1 disaster, the determination of the Apollo program never wavered. NASA remained steadfast in its commitment to fulfilling President Kennedy's vision of landing a man on the moon before the end of the 1960s, and the agency redoubled its efforts to overcome the obstacles that stood in its way.

In the months and years following the Apollo 1 tragedy, NASA undertook a comprehensive review of the Apollo spacecraft's design, manufacturing processes, and operational procedures. The agency implemented a series of corrective actions and safety improvements to address the deficiencies identified by the accident investigation, ensuring that future Apollo missions would be conducted with the highest standards of safety and reliability.

The resolve of the Apollo program was put to the test once again in the aftermath of the Apollo 13 mission, when an oxygen tank explosion crippled the spacecraft en route to the moon. Through ingenuity, resourcefulness, and sheer determination, the crew and mission control worked together to overcome the crisis and safely return the astronauts to Earth—a testament to the indomitable spirit of exploration that defined the Apollo program.

As the 1960s drew to a close, the Apollo program entered its final phase with a series of historic lunar landing missions. Apollo 11, commanded by Neil Armstrong, successfully landed on the moon on July 20, 1969, fulfilling President Kennedy's vision and marking a monumental achievement in human history.

In the chapters that follow, we will delve deeper into the epic saga of the Apollo program, exploring the triumphs and tribulations of humanity's first steps on the lunar surface. We will examine the technological marvels and human dramas that unfolded along the way, and reflect on the enduring legacy of Apollo's journey to the moon.

Chapter 4: Race to the Moon

The race to the moon between the United States and the Soviet Union was one of the defining competitions of the 20th century. Fueled by Cold War tensions and ideological rivalry, the quest to conquer the lunar frontier became a symbol of national pride and technological prowess. This chapter explores the intense competition between the two superpowers, the successes and failures of the Soviet lunar missions, and the immense pressure on NASA to succeed in the Apollo missions.

Intense Competition Between the United States and the Soviet Union:

The rivalry between the United States and the Soviet Union in the realm of space exploration began in earnest with the launch of Sputnik 1 by the Soviet Union in October 1957. The successful launch of the world's first artificial satellite caught the United States off guard and sent shockwaves through the Western world, sparking fears of Soviet technological superiority and prompting a dramatic escalation in the space race.

In response to the Soviet challenge, the United States redoubled its efforts to catch up and surpass its Cold War rival in the field of space exploration. President Dwight D. Eisenhower established NASA in 1958 to coordinate American efforts in space, and the agency quickly set about developing the technology and infrastructure needed to compete with the Soviet Union on equal footing.

The Soviet Union, meanwhile, continued to achieve a series of significant milestones in space exploration throughout the 1960s, further fueling the sense of urgency and competition between the two superpowers. In 1959, the Soviets scored another major victory with the successful launch of Luna 1, the first spacecraft to escape Earth's gravitational pull and venture into deep space.

The following year, the Soviet Union made history once again with the launch of Luna 2, which became the first spacecraft to impact the moon's surface. Luna 2's successful mission demonstrated the Soviet Union's ability to achieve precision lunar targeting—a critical milestone in the quest to land a spacecraft on the moon.

The pressure on NASA to succeed in the Apollo missions:

Against the backdrop of Soviet successes in space, NASA faced mounting pressure to demonstrate American technological prowess and achieve President John F. Kennedy's ambitious goal of landing a man on the moon before the end of the 1960s. The Apollo program, NASA's flagship initiative aimed at achieving this goal, represented a monumental undertaking that would test the agency's capabilities to their limits.

The Apollo program faced numerous technical, logistical, and political challenges from the outset, including the development of the Saturn V rocket, the design and testing of the Apollo spacecraft, and the selection and training of astronauts for lunar missions. Each step of the Apollo program required meticulous planning, precision engineering, and unwavering dedication to the goal of reaching the moon.

The pressure on NASA to succeed in the Apollo missions was further intensified by the Soviet Union's continued progress in space exploration. In 1961, the Soviets achieved another significant milestone with the launch of Yuri Gagarin, the first human in space. Gagarin's historic flight underscored the Soviet Union's lead in the space race and heightened the sense of urgency within NASA to catch up and surpass its Cold War rival.

Throughout the 1960s, NASA worked tirelessly to overcome the myriad technical and logistical challenges of the Apollo program. From the development of the Saturn V rocket—the most powerful rocket ever built—to the rigorous testing and simulation of lunar landing procedures, every aspect of the Apollo missions was carefully planned and executed with the utmost precision.

The Apollo 1 tragedy, which claimed the lives of astronauts Gus Grissom, Ed White, and Roger Chaffee in 1967, served as a stark reminder of the risks inherent in space exploration and the need for unwavering commitment to safety and reliability. Despite the setback, NASA remained determined to press forward with the Apollo program and achieve President Kennedy's vision of landing a man on the moon.

As the 1960s drew to a close, NASA's efforts began to bear fruit with a series of successful Apollo missions that laid the groundwork for the historic lunar landings to come. Apollo 8, the first manned mission to orbit the moon, launched in December 1968 and provided invaluable insights into the lunar environment and the challenges of lunar navigation.

In July 1969, NASA achieved its crowning achievement with the successful landing of Apollo 11 on the moon's surface. Astronauts Neil Armstrong and Buzz Aldrin became the first humans to set foot on the lunar surface, fulfilling President Kennedy's vision and marking a historic milestone in human history.

The Soviet Union's lunar missions:

While the United States ultimately won the race to the moon with the Apollo 11 mission, the Soviet Union also made significant contributions to lunar exploration with its own series of Luna missions. Throughout the 1960s and 1970s, the Soviet Union launched a total of 24 Luna missions to study the moon's surface, conduct scientific experiments, and pave the way for future manned lunar missions.

The Luna missions achieved a number of notable milestones, including the first successful soft landing on the moon by Luna 9 in 1966 and the first robotic lunar rover deployment by Luna 17 in 1970. These achievements demonstrated the Soviet Union's technical capabilities and commitment to lunar exploration, even as the United States took the lead in manned lunar missions.

Despite these successes, the Soviet Union ultimately fell short in its quest to land a man on the moon. The Soviet lunar program faced numerous setbacks and technical challenges, including the loss of several spacecraft and the deaths of cosmonauts in accidents during testing. In the end, the United States emerged victorious in the race to the moon, cementing its place as the leader in space exploration and leaving a lasting legacy of scientific achievement and human exploration on the lunar surface.

In the chapters that follow, we will delve deeper into the epic saga of the Apollo program, exploring the triumphs and tribulations of humanity's first steps on the lunar surface. We will examine the technological marvels and human dramas that unfolded along the way, and reflect on the enduring legacy of the race to the moon.

Chapter 5: Apollo 8 and the First Lunar Orbit

The Apollo 8 mission stands as a historic milestone in human space exploration, marking the first time that astronauts ventured beyond Earth's orbit and orbited the moon. This chapter delves into the significance of the Apollo 8 mission, the iconic "Earthrise" photograph captured during the mission, and the technological and psychological challenges faced by the crew during their journey to the moon.

The Historic Mission of Apollo 8:

Apollo 8, launched on December 21, 1968, was the second crewed mission of NASA's Apollo program and the first to leave Earth's orbit. Commanded by veteran astronaut Frank Borman, with command module pilot James Lovell and lunar module pilot William Anders, Apollo 8 aimed to test the capabilities of the Apollo spacecraft in lunar orbit and pave the way for future manned lunar landings.

The mission began with a flawless launch atop a Saturn V rocket from Kennedy Space Center in Florida. As Apollo 8 hurtled through space towards the moon, the crew experienced the awe-inspiring sensation of leaving Earth's gravitational pull behind—a feat never before accomplished by human beings.

After a three-day journey, Apollo 8 entered lunar orbit on December 24, 1968, becoming the first spacecraft to circle the moon. The crew conducted a series of orbits around the lunar surface, gathering valuable data on the moon's terrain and geology and testing the spacecraft's navigation and communication systems in the harsh environment of space.

The crew of Apollo 8 also made history with a live television broadcast from lunar orbit, during which they shared their observations and experiences with viewers around the world. The broadcast captivated audiences and brought the wonder and excitement of space exploration into living rooms across the globe, inspiring a new generation to dream of reaching for the stars.

The Iconic "Earthrise" Photograph:

One of the most iconic moments of the Apollo 8 mission came during the crew's fourth orbit of the moon, when they captured a breathtaking photograph of Earth rising above the lunar horizon. The image, known as "Earthrise," quickly became one of the most famous photographs in history and symbolized the fragility and beauty of our planet against the vast expanse of space.

The "Earthrise" photograph had a profound impact on humanity's perception of our place in the cosmos. For the first time, people around the world were able to see Earth from the perspective of astronauts orbiting the moon—a tiny blue and white oasis suspended in the blackness of space. The image underscored the interconnectedness of all life on Earth and the need to preserve and protect our planet for future generations.

The Technological and Psychological Challenges:

The Apollo 8 mission presented a host of technological and psychological challenges for the crew, as they ventured farther from Earth than any human beings had ever traveled before. The crew faced the harsh realities of space travel, including the isolation and confinement of living in a cramped spacecraft for days on end, the constant threat of radiation and micrometeoroid impacts, and the intense pressure of navigating through uncharted territory.

The crew also grappled with the psychological effects of being cut off from the familiar comforts of home and family for an extended period of time. Despite the rigorous training and preparation, the mental and emotional strain of living and working in the harsh environment of space took its toll on the crew, testing their resilience and determination to complete their mission.

Throughout their journey to the moon and back, the crew of Apollo 8 demonstrated extraordinary courage, skill, and teamwork in the face of adversity. They overcame the challenges of space travel with grace and determination, inspiring generations of future astronauts to follow in their footsteps and explore the mysteries of the cosmos.

In the years since the Apollo 8 mission, the legacy of its historic journey to the moon has continued to inspire and captivate people around the world. The "Earthrise" photograph remains a powerful reminder of the fragility and beauty of our planet, and the courage and ingenuity of the men and women who ventured into the unknown to explore the cosmos. As humanity looks towards the future of space exploration, the spirit of Apollo 8 serves as a beacon of hope and inspiration for generations to come.

Chapter 6: Preparing for Landing

The preparations for the historic Apollo 11 moon landing were a culmination of years of intensive planning, testing, and training by NASA and its team of scientists, engineers, and astronauts. This chapter delves into the Apollo missions leading up to the moon landing, including Apollo 9 and Apollo 10, the rigorous tests and simulations conducted to ensure a successful landing, and the selection and training of the Apollo 11 crew.

Apollo Missions Leading Up to the Moon Landing:

Before embarking on the historic Apollo 11 mission, NASA conducted a series of precursor missions to test the Apollo spacecraft and lunar module in Earth orbit and prepare for the challenges of landing on the moon. Two of the key missions leading up to Apollo 11 were Apollo 9 and Apollo 10.

Apollo 9, launched on March 3, 1969, was the first mission to test the complete Apollo spacecraft in Earth orbit. Commanded by James McDivitt, with command module pilot David Scott and lunar module pilot Rusty Schweickart, Apollo 9 conducted a series of critical tests of the lunar module's propulsion, navigation, and docking capabilities.

During the mission, the crew separated the command module from the lunar module and performed a series of maneuvers to simulate the procedures required for a lunar landing. They also conducted a spacewalk to test the feasibility of extravehicular activities (EVAs) on the moon's surface. Apollo 9 successfully demonstrated the functionality and performance of the Apollo spacecraft in Earth orbit, paving the way for future lunar missions.

Apollo 10, launched on May 18, 1969, was a dress rehearsal for the Apollo 11 moon landing, with the mission objectives focused on testing the lunar module in lunar orbit. Commanded by Tom Stafford, with command module pilot John Young and lunar module pilot Gene Cernan, Apollo 10 performed a series of maneuvers to rendezvous and dock with the lunar module in lunar orbit.

During the mission, the crew brought the lunar module to within 50,000 feet of the lunar surface—the closest approach to the moon achieved by any spacecraft up to that point. They also tested the lunar module's descent and ascent engines in lunar orbit and conducted a simulated descent to within 10 miles of the lunar surface before returning to the command module for the journey back to Earth. Apollo 10 provided invaluable data and experience that would prove crucial for the success of the Apollo 11 mission.

Tests and Simulations:

In preparation for the Apollo 11 moon landing, NASA conducted a comprehensive series of tests and simulations to ensure that every aspect of the mission was meticulously planned and executed. These tests and simulations encompassed a wide range of scenarios and contingencies, from lunar module descent and ascent to lunar surface operations and crew safety procedures.

One of the most critical tests conducted by NASA was the Lunar Landing Training Vehicle (LLTV) program, which used a series of specialized training vehicles to simulate the lunar module's descent and landing on the moon's surface. Astronauts trained extensively in the LLTVs to familiarize themselves with the handling characteristics of the lunar module and refine their piloting skills for the challenging landing maneuver.

NASA also conducted a series of simulated lunar surface missions, known as geology field trips, to train astronauts in the scientific techniques and equipment they would use to explore the lunar landscape. These field trips involved realistic simulations of lunar terrain and geological features, allowing astronauts to practice collecting rock samples and conducting experiments in simulated lunar gravity conditions.

In addition to technical training, NASA also focused on preparing the Apollo 11 crew for the psychological and physiological challenges of the moon landing mission. Astronauts underwent rigorous physical fitness training and medical evaluations to ensure they were in peak condition for the demands of space travel and lunar exploration. They also participated in extensive briefings and debriefings to review mission objectives, procedures, and contingencies.

The Selection and Training of the Apollo 11 Crew:

The selection of the Apollo 11 crew was a carefully orchestrated process, with NASA choosing three veteran astronauts with extensive experience in spaceflight and mission leadership roles. The crew of Apollo 11 consisted of:

- Neil Armstrong, commander of Apollo 11 and the first human to set foot on the moon.

- Buzz Aldrin, lunar module pilot of Apollo 11 and the second human to walk on the moon.

- Michael Collins, command module pilot of Apollo 11, who remained in lunar orbit while Armstrong and Aldrin explored the moon's surface.

Each member of the Apollo 11 crew brought unique skills, expertise, and experience to the mission, making them ideally suited to the challenges of the moon landing. Neil Armstrong, a seasoned test pilot and engineer, was chosen for his calm demeanor, exceptional piloting skills, and leadership qualities. Buzz Aldrin, a former Air Force pilot and astronaut, was selected for his technical expertise, scientific acumen, and ability to perform complex tasks in space. Michael Collins, a skilled astronaut and pilot, was chosen for his proficiency in spacecraft operations, navigation, and communication.

In the years leading up to the Apollo 11 mission, the crew underwent rigorous training and preparation to ensure they were fully prepared for the challenges of lunar exploration. They participated in a wide range of technical, scientific, and operational training activities, including simulations of lunar surface operations, spacecraft maneuvers, and emergency procedures.

The crew of Apollo 11 also worked closely with NASA engineers, scientists, and mission planners to refine mission objectives, procedures, and contingency plans. They conducted countless hours of simulations and rehearsals to familiarize themselves with every aspect of the mission and develop strategies for overcoming potential challenges and obstacles.

Despite the immense pressure and scrutiny surrounding the Apollo 11 mission, the crew remained focused, disciplined, and determined to succeed. Their unwavering commitment to the goal of landing a man on the moon and returning him safely to Earth served as a source of inspiration and motivation for the entire nation.

As the launch date for Apollo 11 approached, anticipation and excitement reached a fever pitch as people around the world eagerly awaited humanity's first steps on the lunar surface. The stage was set for one of the most historic and momentous events in human history—the Apollo 11 moon landing.

In the chapters that follow, we will delve deeper into the epic saga of the Apollo 11 mission, exploring the triumphs and tribulations of humanity's first steps on the lunar surface. We will examine the technological marvels and human dramas that unfolded along the way, and reflect on the enduring legacy of Apollo's journey to the moon.

Chapter 7: Countdown to Launch

The countdown to the launch of the Apollo 11 mission was a culmination of years of preparation, testing, and anticipation. This chapter delves into the final preparations for the historic mission, the tension and anticipation surrounding the launch, and the global audience that watched as humanity prepared to take its first steps on another celestial body.

Final Preparations for the Apollo 11 Mission:

In the weeks leading up to the launch of Apollo 11, NASA and its team of engineers, scientists, and astronauts worked tirelessly to ensure that every aspect of the mission was meticulously planned and executed. The spacecraft underwent final checks and inspections, and the crew conducted last-minute training and simulations to prepare for the challenges of the mission.

The Apollo 11 spacecraft consisted of three main components: the command module Columbia, the lunar module Eagle, and the Saturn V rocket that would propel them into space. Each component underwent rigorous testing and validation to ensure that it met the stringent requirements for spaceflight and lunar landing.

The crew of Apollo 11—Commander Neil Armstrong, Lunar Module Pilot Buzz Aldrin, and Command Module Pilot Michael Collins—participated in a series of final briefings and rehearsals to review mission objectives, procedures, and contingency plans. They familiarized themselves with the spacecraft systems and emergency protocols, preparing themselves mentally and physically for the demands of space travel and lunar exploration.

In addition to technical preparations, NASA also focused on ensuring the health and well-being of the crew during the mission. The astronauts underwent extensive medical evaluations and physical fitness assessments to ensure they were in peak condition for the rigors of spaceflight. They also received vaccinations and medical treatments to protect against potential health hazards in space.

As the launch date approached, anticipation and excitement mounted among the crew and the entire NASA team. The realization that they were on the cusp of making history—to be the first humans to set foot on the moon—filled them with a sense of awe and responsibility that drove them to succeed against all odds.

The Tension and Anticipation Surrounding the Launch:

On the morning of July 16, 1969, the world watched with bated breath as the countdown to the launch of Apollo 11 began. Millions of people around the globe tuned in to live television broadcasts and radio transmissions, eagerly awaiting the historic moment when humanity would embark on its greatest adventure yet.

At Kennedy Space Center in Florida, the launch pad was a hive of activity as engineers, technicians, and support personnel made final preparations for the mission. The Saturn V rocket stood tall on the launch pad, its gleaming white exterior towering over the surrounding landscape, a testament to human ingenuity and determination.

As the countdown clock ticked inexorably towards zero, the tension and anticipation reached a fever pitch. Every moment felt like an eternity as the world held its breath, waiting for the moment when the mighty Saturn V rocket would ignite its engines and propel Apollo 11 towards the heavens.

Finally, at 9:32 a.m. Eastern Daylight Time, the moment of truth arrived. With a deafening roar and a blinding flash of light, the engines of the Saturn V rocket ignited, sending plumes of smoke and flames billowing into the sky. Slowly but inexorably, the massive rocket lifted off from the launch pad, carrying Apollo 11 and its crew on the journey of a lifetime.

The global audience watching as humanity prepared to take its first steps on another celestial body:

As Apollo 11 soared into the sky, the eyes of the world were fixed on the live television broadcasts and radio transmissions that brought the historic launch into living rooms, schools, and public spaces around the globe. Millions of people followed the progress of the mission with rapt attention, captivated by the drama and excitement of humanity's first voyage to the moon.

In the United States, crowds gathered in public squares, parks, and auditoriums to watch the launch on large screens set up for the occasion. Families huddled around television sets, holding their breath as they witnessed the historic moment unfold before their eyes. Schools canceled classes so students could watch the launch live, recognizing the educational significance of the event and the inspiration it provided to future generations of scientists, engineers, and explorers.

Beyond the United States, the launch of Apollo 11 captured the imagination of people from every corner of the globe. In Europe, Asia, Africa, and South America, millions of people gathered around radios and televisions to witness the historic moment when humanity took its first steps towards the stars.

In countries like the Soviet Union, where the space race had sparked intense competition and national pride, the launch of Apollo 11 was met with a mixture of awe and admiration. Despite their own achievements in space exploration, many Soviet citizens watched with fascination as their Cold War rival embarked on this historic mission, recognizing the significance of humanity's collective journey to the moon.

As Apollo 11 continued on its journey to the moon, the global audience remained glued to their screens, following every twist and turn of the mission with breathless anticipation. For eight days, the world watched as the crew of Apollo 11 ventured into the unknown, overcoming challenges and obstacles with courage and determination.

In the chapters that follow, we will delve deeper into the epic saga of the Apollo 11 mission, exploring the triumphs and tribulations of humanity's first steps on the lunar surface. We will examine the technological marvels and human dramas that unfolded along the way, and reflect on the enduring legacy of Apollo's journey to the moon.

Chapter 8: Tranquility Base

The journey of Apollo 11 to the moon and the historic descent to the lunar surface marked a pivotal moment in human history—a moment that would be forever etched in the annals of exploration and achievement. This chapter delves into the awe-inspiring journey of Apollo 11 to the moon, the nail-biting descent to the lunar surface, Neil Armstrong's famous words as he stepped onto the moon, and the profound significance of the moon landing for humanity and its impact on the world.

The Journey of Apollo 11 to the Moon:

Following its flawless launch from Kennedy Space Center on July 16, 1969, Apollo 11 embarked on a historic journey to the moon. The crew—Commander Neil Armstrong, Lunar Module Pilot Buzz Aldrin, and Command Module Pilot Michael Collins—spent three days traversing the vast expanse of space, hurtling through the void at speeds of over 24,000 miles per hour.

As Apollo 11 approached the moon, the crew prepared for the critical maneuver known as lunar orbit insertion (LOI), which would place the spacecraft into orbit around the moon. On July 19, 1969, the command module Columbia fired its main engine to slow down and enter lunar orbit—a maneuver executed with flawless precision by the skilled crew.

For the next day, Apollo 11 orbited the moon, conducting observations and photography of potential landing sites while finalizing preparations for the historic descent to the lunar surface. On July 20, 1969, the crew of Apollo 11 prepared to make history as they descended towards the moon aboard the lunar module Eagle.

The Descent to the Lunar Surface:

As the lunar module Eagle separated from the command module Columbia and began its descent towards the moon's surface, the tension in Mission Control and around the world reached a fever pitch. Every second felt like an eternity as Neil Armstrong and Buzz Aldrin guided the spacecraft towards their designated landing site in the Sea of Tranquility.

As Eagle approached the lunar surface, the crew encountered a series of unexpected challenges, including a boulder-strewn landscape and a computer alarm triggered by an overload of data. With split-second decision-making and nerves of steel, Neil Armstrong took manual control of the spacecraft and piloted it to a safe landing site, narrowly avoiding disaster and cementing his place in history as one of humanity's greatest heroes.

At 4:17 p.m. Eastern Daylight Time on July 20, 1969, the world held its breath as Neil Armstrong's voice crackled over the radio, announcing the historic moment when Eagle touched down on the lunar surface. "Houston, Tranquility Base here. The Eagle has landed," Armstrong declared, his words echoing through the halls of Mission Control and reverberating in the hearts of people around the world.

Neil Armstrong's Famous Words:

As Neil Armstrong prepared to take humanity's first steps on the moon, he uttered the now-famous words that would echo throughout history: "That's one small step for [a] man, one giant leap for mankind." With those iconic words, Armstrong stepped off the ladder of the lunar module and onto the surface of the moon, fulfilling President John F. Kennedy's vision and capturing the imagination of people around the world.

As Buzz Aldrin followed Armstrong down the ladder and onto the lunar surface, the two astronauts set about conducting scientific experiments, collecting rock samples, and planting the American flag—a symbol of human achievement and exploration in the vast expanse of space. They also placed a plaque on the lunar surface bearing the inscription: "Here men from the planet Earth first set foot upon the moon July 1969, A.D. We came in peace for all mankind."

The Significance of the Moon Landing for Humanity:

The moon landing of Apollo 11 was more than just a technological achievement—it was a defining moment in human history that transcended national boundaries and united people around the world in awe and wonder. For the first time, human beings had ventured beyond the confines of Earth and set foot on another celestial body—a feat that had been the stuff of dreams and science fiction for centuries.

The significance of the moon landing extended far beyond the realm of space exploration, touching the hearts and minds of people from every walk of life. It symbolized humanity's indomitable spirit of curiosity, exploration, and discovery, and served as a beacon of hope and inspiration for generations to come.

The moon landing also had profound implications for science, technology, and the future of human space exploration. It provided invaluable data and insights into the geology, atmosphere, and history of the moon, paving the way for future lunar missions and the establishment of permanent human settlements on the lunar surface.

Moreover, the moon landing of Apollo 11 sparked a renewed sense of optimism and possibility in the hearts of people around the world. It demonstrated the power of human ingenuity and cooperation to overcome seemingly insurmountable challenges and achieve the impossible.

In the decades since the historic landing of Apollo 11, humanity has continued to push the boundaries of exploration and discovery, venturing deeper into the cosmos in search of answers to the fundamental questions of existence. The legacy of Apollo 11 lives on in the hearts and minds of people everywhere, serving as a reminder of what can be accomplished when we dare to dream big and reach for the stars.

Chapter 9: Exploring the Lunar Surface

The exploration of the lunar surface by Neil Armstrong and Buzz Aldrin during their time on the moon was a defining moment in human history—one that would forever change our understanding of the cosmos and our place within it. This chapter delves into the activities of Armstrong and Aldrin during their historic moonwalk, the scientific experiments conducted and samples collected, and the challenges and triumphs of lunar exploration.

Activities of Neil Armstrong and Buzz Aldrin:

After landing the lunar module Eagle on the surface of the moon on July 20, 1969, Neil Armstrong and Buzz Aldrin prepared to venture outside and become the first humans to set foot on another celestial body. Clad in their iconic white spacesuits and equipped with cameras, scientific instruments, and sample collection tools, the two astronauts descended the ladder of the lunar module and stepped onto the dusty surface of the moon.

As they explored the lunar landscape, Armstrong and Aldrin conducted a series of scientific experiments, collected rock and soil samples, and took photographs and video footage to document their historic journey. They also deployed a series of scientific instruments, including seismometers and reflectors, to study the moon's geology, atmosphere, and magnetic field.

One of the primary objectives of the Apollo 11 mission was to gather geological data and samples from the lunar surface to better understand the moon's origins and evolution. Armstrong and Aldrin carefully selected rocks and soil samples from various locations around the landing site, using specialized tools to collect and document each specimen.

In addition to their scientific duties, Armstrong and Aldrin also took time to explore the lunar landscape and marvel at the breathtaking vistas stretching out before them. They bounded across the dusty surface of the moon, leaving footprints that would remain undisturbed for thousands of years, and paused to take in the otherworldly beauty of their surroundings.

Scientific Experiments and Samples Collected:

During their time on the moon, Armstrong and Aldrin conducted a wide range of scientific experiments and collected over 47 pounds (21.5 kilograms) of rock and soil samples for analysis back on Earth. These samples provided invaluable insights into the geology, chemistry, and history of the moon, shedding light on its origins and evolution over billions of years.

One of the key experiments conducted by Armstrong and Aldrin was the deployment of a passive seismic experiment package, which consisted of four seismometers placed at different locations around the landing site. These seismometers measured the moon's seismic activity, providing valuable data on its internal structure and composition.

Another important experiment conducted by Armstrong and Aldrin was the deployment of a laser ranging retroreflector, which consisted of a series of mirrors designed to reflect laser beams sent from Earth. This experiment allowed scientists to accurately measure the distance between the Earth and the moon with unprecedented precision, providing valuable data for future lunar missions and scientific research.

In addition to these experiments, Armstrong and Aldrin also collected a wide range of rock and soil samples from the lunar surface. These samples included basalts, breccias, and regolith—fragments of rock and soil that had been blasted from the moon's surface by meteorite impacts and other geological processes.

Each sample was carefully cataloged and stored in airtight containers to prevent contamination and preserve their pristine condition for analysis back on Earth. Scientists would spend years studying these samples, using a variety of analytical techniques to unravel the mysteries of the moon's geological history and formation.

Challenges and Triumphs of Lunar Exploration:

The exploration of the lunar surface presented numerous challenges and obstacles for Armstrong and Aldrin, from the harsh lunar environment to the complexities of operating in microgravity. One of the primary challenges they faced was navigating the uneven and treacherous terrain of the moon, which was littered with boulders, craters, and dust.

Despite these challenges, Armstrong and Aldrin pressed on with determination and perseverance, overcoming obstacles with skill and ingenuity. They carefully maneuvered around obstacles and hazards, using their training and experience to navigate the lunar landscape with precision and grace.

Another challenge faced by Armstrong and Aldrin was the limited mobility and visibility afforded by their bulky spacesuits and helmets. The stiff, pressurized suits restricted their movements and made it difficult to perform tasks requiring fine motor skills, such as collecting rock samples and setting up scientific instruments.

Despite these challenges, Armstrong and Aldrin successfully completed all of their planned tasks and objectives, demonstrating the resilience and adaptability of the human spirit in the face of adversity. Their triumphs on the lunar surface inspired people around the world and solidified their place in history as pioneers of space exploration.

As Armstrong and Aldrin prepared to return to the lunar module Eagle and rendezvous with Michael Collins in lunar orbit, they reflected on the magnitude of their achievements and the profound impact of their journey on humanity. They had accomplished what many thought impossible, proving that with determination, courage, and ingenuity, humanity could overcome any obstacle and reach for the stars.

In the decades since the historic moonwalk of Apollo 11, the legacy of Neil Armstrong and Buzz Aldrin has continued to inspire and captivate people around the world. Their footsteps on the lunar surface serve as a symbol of human achievement and exploration, reminding us of the boundless potential of the human spirit to reach beyond the confines of Earth and explore the wonders of the cosmos.

Chapter 10: Return to Earth

The return journey of Apollo 11 from the lunar surface to Earth marked the culmination of one of humanity's greatest achievements—the first manned mission to land on the moon. This chapter explores the ascent from the lunar surface, the rendezvous with the command module, the journey back to Earth, and the celebrations that awaited the astronauts upon their return. It also delves into reflections on the significance of the moon landing and its lasting legacy.

Ascent from the Lunar Surface and Rendezvous with the Command Module:

After spending approximately 21 hours on the lunar surface, Neil Armstrong and Buzz Aldrin prepared to leave Tranquility Base and rejoin Michael Collins in the command module Columbia. Their ascent from the lunar surface was a critical maneuver that required flawless execution to ensure a safe return to lunar orbit.

On July 21, 1969, Armstrong and Aldrin entered the lunar module Eagle and initiated the ascent sequence. With a burst of thrust from the ascent engine, Eagle lifted off from the surface of the moon, leaving behind the desolate landscape of the lunar surface and beginning its journey back to lunar orbit.

As Eagle ascended towards lunar orbit, Armstrong and Aldrin carefully monitored the spacecraft's systems and trajectory, making minor adjustments as needed to ensure a smooth ascent. Meanwhile, Michael Collins remained in lunar orbit aboard the command module Columbia, anxiously awaiting the rendezvous with his fellow astronauts.

After a series of orbital maneuvers and trajectory corrections, Eagle successfully rendezvoused with Columbia in lunar orbit. The two spacecraft docked together, and Armstrong and Aldrin transferred back to Columbia, reuniting with Collins for the journey back to Earth.

The Journey Back to Earth:

With the crew of Apollo 11 safely reunited aboard Columbia, the spacecraft prepared to depart lunar orbit and begin the long journey back to Earth. On July 21, 1969, Columbia fired its main engine to break free from lunar orbit and set a course for home.

As Columbia hurtled through space towards Earth, the crew settled into their routine of daily tasks, scientific experiments, and navigation duties. They monitored the spacecraft's systems, conducted routine maintenance, and communicated with Mission Control as they made their way across the vast expanse of space.

Despite the immense distance and the challenges of operating in the harsh environment of space, the journey back to Earth proceeded smoothly, with the crew of Apollo 11 working together with precision and efficiency to ensure a safe return.

On July 24, 1969, after a journey of approximately 240,000 miles (386,000 kilometers), Columbia reentered Earth's atmosphere, blazing through the sky at speeds of over 25,000 miles per hour (40,000 kilometers per hour). As the spacecraft descended towards the Pacific Ocean, parachutes deployed to slow its descent, and Columbia splashed down safely in the ocean.

The crew of Apollo 11 emerged from their spacecraft, greeted by the sight of recovery helicopters and the cheers of the recovery team aboard the USS Hornet aircraft carrier. They were quickly hoisted aboard the recovery helicopter and flown to the deck of the USS Hornet, where they were greeted with a heroes' welcome and congratulated for their historic achievement.

Celebrations and Reflections:

As the crew of Apollo 11 returned to Earth and began the process of quarantine and debriefing, they were welcomed as heroes and hailed as pioneers of space exploration. Parades, ceremonies, and celebrations were held in their honor across the United States and around the world, as people rejoiced in the success of humanity's first manned mission to the moon.

The crew of Apollo 11 reflected on the significance of their journey and the profound impact it had on humanity. They spoke of the awe-inspiring beauty of the lunar landscape, the exhilaration of walking on the moon, and the sense of camaraderie and unity that had characterized their mission.

Neil Armstrong, Buzz Aldrin, and Michael Collins spoke eloquently about the importance of exploration, discovery, and the pursuit of knowledge. They emphasized the need for continued investment in space exploration and scientific research, recognizing the potential of space exploration to inspire future generations and unlock the mysteries of the cosmos.

As the world celebrated the success of Apollo 11, people everywhere marveled at the achievements of Armstrong, Aldrin, and Collins, and the countless men and women who had worked tirelessly behind the scenes to make the mission a reality. The moon landing of Apollo 11 had captured the imagination of people around the world and inspired a renewed sense of wonder and curiosity about the universe.

In the decades since the historic mission of Apollo 11, the legacy of Neil Armstrong, Buzz Aldrin, and Michael Collins has continued to inspire and captivate people around the world. Their courage, ingenuity, and pioneering spirit serve as a reminder of what can be accomplished when humanity dares to dream big and reach for the stars. As we look towards the future of space exploration, we carry with us the lessons and achievements of Apollo 11, and the knowledge that the human spirit knows no bounds.

Chapter 11: Post-Moon Landing

The aftermath of Apollo 11 and its historic moon landing reverberated around the world, leaving an indelible mark on human history and igniting a new era of exploration and discovery. This chapter explores the immediate aftermath of Apollo 11 and its impact on space exploration, the continuation of the Apollo program and subsequent moon missions, and the technological advancements and scientific discoveries that resulted from the moon landing.

The Aftermath of Apollo 11 and its Impact on Space Exploration:

The successful completion of Apollo 11 and humanity's first steps on the moon marked the culmination of years of effort, sacrifice, and determination by thousands of scientists, engineers, and astronauts. It was a moment of triumph and jubilation for the United States and a testament to the power of human ingenuity and perseverance.

In the immediate aftermath of Apollo 11, the world celebrated the historic achievement of Neil Armstrong, Buzz Aldrin, and Michael Collins, hailing them as heroes and pioneers of space exploration. Parades, ceremonies, and celebrations were held in their honor across the United States and around the world, as people rejoiced in the success of humanity's first manned mission to the moon.

The legacy of Apollo 11 extended far beyond the confines of Earth, inspiring future generations of scientists, engineers, and explorers to reach for the stars and pursue their dreams of space exploration. It sparked a renewed sense of optimism and possibility in the hearts and minds of people around the world, igniting a new era of exploration and discovery.

One of the most significant impacts of Apollo 11 was its role in galvanizing public support for space exploration and scientific research.

The success of the mission demonstrated the potential of human spaceflight to push the boundaries of knowledge and inspire future generations to explore the cosmos.

The Continuation of the Apollo Program and Subsequent Moon Missions:

Following the success of Apollo 11, NASA continued to push forward with its ambitious plans for lunar exploration, launching a series of follow-up missions to build on the achievements of Apollo 11 and expand our understanding of the moon.

Apollo 12, launched on November 14, 1969, was the second manned mission to land on the moon. Commanded by Charles "Pete" Conrad, with Alan L. Bean as the lunar module pilot and Richard F. Gordon as the command module pilot, Apollo 12 achieved a pinpoint landing in the Ocean of Storms, paving the way for future manned missions to explore new regions of the lunar surface.

Subsequent Apollo missions, including Apollo 13, Apollo 14, Apollo 15, Apollo 16, and Apollo 17, continued to push the boundaries of lunar exploration, conducting scientific experiments, collecting rock and soil samples, and expanding our knowledge of the moon's geology, atmosphere, and magnetic field.

Apollo 13, launched on April 11, 1970, famously experienced an oxygen tank explosion en route to the moon, forcing the crew to abort their mission and return to Earth. Despite the harrowing ordeal, the crew of Apollo 13—Commander James A. Lovell, Command Module Pilot John L. Swigert, and Lunar Module Pilot Fred W. Haise—returned safely to Earth, demonstrating the resilience and adaptability of the human spirit in the face of adversity.

Technological Advancements and Scientific Discoveries Resulting from the Moon Landing:

The moon landing of Apollo 11 represented a triumph of human ingenuity and engineering prowess, pushing the boundaries of technology and innovation to achieve the seemingly impossible. It spurred a wave of technological advancements and scientific discoveries that continue to shape our understanding of the universe.

One of the most significant technological advancements resulting from the moon landing was the development of the Saturn V rocket—the most powerful rocket ever built. The Saturn V played a critical role in enabling the Apollo missions to reach the moon and return safely to Earth, demonstrating the potential of human spaceflight to explore the cosmos.

The moon landing also paved the way for advances in space exploration technology, including spacecraft design, propulsion systems, life support systems, and navigation and communication systems. These technological innovations have laid the foundation for future manned and unmanned missions to explore the solar system and beyond.

In addition to technological advancements, the moon landing of Apollo 11 yielded a wealth of scientific discoveries that have transformed our understanding of the moon and its place in the solar system. The rock and soil samples collected during the Apollo missions have provided valuable insights into the moon's geological history, composition, and origins, shedding light on its formation and evolution over billions of years.

The scientific experiments conducted on the lunar surface, including seismic studies, laser ranging experiments, and measurements of the moon's magnetic field, have expanded our knowledge of the moon's internal structure and processes, deepening our understanding of the fundamental principles governing the formation and evolution of planetary bodies.

Moreover, the legacy of Apollo 11 extends beyond the realm of science and technology, inspiring future generations to pursue careers in STEM fields and fostering a sense of wonder and curiosity about the universe. The moon landing of Apollo 11 serves as a testament to the power of human exploration and discovery, reminding us of the boundless potential of the human spirit to reach beyond the confines of Earth and explore the wonders of the cosmos.

In the decades since the historic mission of Apollo 11, the legacy of Neil Armstrong, Buzz Aldrin, Michael Collins, and the thousands of men and women who made the mission possible has continued to inspire and captivate people around the world. Their achievements serve as a reminder of what can be accomplished when humanity dares to dream big and reach for the stars. As we look towards the future of space exploration, we carry with us the lessons and achievements of Apollo 11, and the knowledge that the human spirit knows no bounds.

Chapter 12: Cultural Impact

The moon landing of Apollo 11 transcended the realm of science and technology, leaving an indelible mark on human culture and society that continues to resonate to this day. This chapter explores the worldwide reaction to the moon landing and its portrayal in the media, the role of the moon landing in shaping national and international identity, and the cultural legacy of Apollo 11 and its influence on art, literature, and popular culture.

Worldwide Reaction to the Moon Landing and its Portrayal in the Media:

The worldwide reaction to the moon landing of Apollo 11 was one of awe, wonder, and jubilation, as people around the globe watched with bated breath as humanity achieved one of its greatest dreams. From the streets of New York City to the villages of rural Africa, millions of people gathered around television sets and radios to witness the historic moment when Neil Armstrong and Buzz Aldrin stepped onto the lunar surface.

In the United States, the moon landing was met with an outpouring of national pride and patriotism, as people from all walks of life celebrated the achievement of American ingenuity and determination. Parades, ceremonies, and celebrations were held in cities and towns across the country, as people waved flags, sang songs, and cheered for the brave astronauts who had made history.

The media played a crucial role in shaping public perceptions of the moon landing, with newspapers, magazines, television networks, and radio stations providing extensive coverage of the historic event. Front-page headlines proclaimed "Man Walks on Moon" in bold letters, while television anchors delivered live broadcasts from Mission Control and the lunar surface, bringing the drama and excitement of the mission into living rooms around the world.

In addition to traditional media outlets, the moon landing of Apollo 11 was also celebrated in popular culture, with songs, films, books, and artwork inspired by the historic event. Musicians penned ballads and anthems paying tribute to the astronauts and their journey to the moon, while filmmakers and authors used the moon landing as a backdrop for tales of adventure, exploration, and discovery.

The Role of the Moon Landing in Shaping National and International Identity:

The moon landing of Apollo 11 played a significant role in shaping national and international identity, serving as a symbol of human achievement and progress that transcended national boundaries and united people around the world in awe and wonder. For the United States, the success of Apollo 11 reaffirmed the nation's status as a global leader in science, technology, and innovation, showcasing the power of American ingenuity and determination to overcome seemingly insurmountable challenges.

In the context of the Cold War rivalry between the United States and the Soviet Union, the moon landing represented a decisive victory for the American space program and a triumph of democracy and freedom over communism and tyranny. It served as a powerful symbol of American exceptionalism and the superiority of the capitalist system, bolstering national pride and confidence in the face of geopolitical competition.

Internationally, the moon landing of Apollo 11 inspired admiration and respect for the United States and its achievements in space exploration, as people around the world looked on with admiration at the courage and determination of the American astronauts. The success of Apollo 11 also fueled aspirations for space exploration and scientific progress in countries around the world, inspiring new generations of scientists, engineers, and explorers to pursue their dreams of reaching for the stars.

The Cultural Legacy of Apollo 11 and its Influence on Art, Literature, and Popular Culture:

The moon landing of Apollo 11 left an enduring cultural legacy that continues to inspire and captivate people around the world, shaping the artistic, literary, and popular culture of the 20th and 21st centuries. From paintings and sculptures to novels and films, the moon landing has been a rich source of inspiration for artists, writers, and creators of all kinds.

In the realm of art, the moon landing has been depicted in countless paintings, sculptures, and mixed-media works that capture the awe-inspiring beauty and majesty of the lunar landscape. Artists like Robert Rauschenberg, Andy Warhol, and Norman Rockwell have created iconic images inspired by the moon landing, while photographers like Ansel Adams and Annie Leibovitz have captured the human drama and emotion of space exploration in their photographs.

In literature, the moon landing has been the subject of countless novels, short stories, and essays that explore the human experience of space travel and the profound impact of the lunar landing on society and culture. Writers like Arthur C. Clarke, Isaac Asimov, and Ray Bradbury have imagined futures where space exploration plays a central role, while poets like Maya Angelou and Langston Hughes have used the moon landing as a metaphor for the triumph of the human spirit.

In popular culture, the moon landing has inspired a wide range of films, television shows, and music that celebrate the spirit of exploration and adventure. Films like "2001: A Space Odyssey," "Apollo 13," and "First Man" have brought the drama and excitement of space exploration to the big screen, while television shows like "Star Trek" and "The X-Files" have explored the possibilities of life beyond Earth.

Moreover, the moon landing has left its mark on popular culture in more subtle ways, influencing fashion, design, and consumer products. From moon-themed fashion collections to lunar-inspired home decor, the imagery and symbolism of the moon landing have permeated every aspect of modern life, serving as a constant reminder of humanity's enduring fascination with the cosmos.

In conclusion, the moon landing of Apollo 11 was a transformative moment in human history that left an indelible mark on culture and society. Its impact continues to resonate to this day, inspiring new generations to reach for the stars and explore the mysteries of the universe. As we look towards the future of space exploration, we carry with us the legacy of Apollo 11 and the knowledge that the human spirit knows no bounds when it comes to exploring the cosmos.

Chapter 13: Looking to the Future

The legacy of Apollo 11 extends far beyond the historic moon landing of 1969, shaping the trajectory of human space exploration and inspiring new generations to reach for the stars. This chapter explores the enduring legacy of Apollo 11 and its impact on future space exploration, the challenges and opportunities of returning to the moon and beyond, and the vision for humanity's future in space exploration.

The Legacy of Apollo 11 and its Impact on Future Space Exploration:

The legacy of Apollo 11 is one of inspiration, innovation, and discovery—a testament to the power of human ingenuity and determination to explore the unknown. The success of Apollo 11 demonstrated what could be accomplished when humanity dared to dream big and push the boundaries of exploration and discovery.

One of the most enduring legacies of Apollo 11 is its role in inspiring future generations of scientists, engineers, and explorers to pursue careers in STEM fields and contribute to the advancement of space exploration. The achievements of Neil Armstrong, Buzz Aldrin, and Michael Collins serve as a constant reminder of what can be accomplished when we work together towards a common goal.

Moreover, the technological advancements and scientific discoveries resulting from the moon landing have laid the foundation for future space exploration missions, providing valuable insights into the challenges and opportunities of exploring the cosmos. The lessons learned from Apollo 11 continue to inform and inspire new generations of space explorers as they embark on the next chapter of humanity's journey into space.

The Challenges and Opportunities of Returning

to the Moon and Beyond:

As humanity looks to the future of space exploration, returning to the moon and beyond presents both challenges and opportunities that will shape the course of human history for generations to come. One of the greatest challenges of returning to the moon is the development of the necessary technology and infrastructure to support long-term human habitation and exploration.

Despite these challenges, returning to the moon also presents a wealth of opportunities for scientific discovery, technological innovation, and international collaboration. The moon is a treasure trove of resources, including water ice, minerals, and rare metals, that could be exploited to support future lunar missions and enable human settlement.

Moreover, the moon serves as a stepping stone for future missions to Mars and beyond, providing a testing ground for new technologies and techniques that will be essential for interplanetary travel. By establishing a permanent human presence on the moon, we can learn valuable lessons about living and working in space that will inform future missions to distant worlds.

The Vision for Humanity's Future in Space Exploration:

As we look to the future of space exploration, the vision for humanity's future is one of exploration, discovery, and collaboration. The moon landing of Apollo 11 was just the beginning of humanity's journey into space, and the possibilities for exploration and discovery are limitless.

One of the key goals of future space exploration missions is to establish a sustainable human presence on the moon and beyond, enabling long-term exploration and scientific research. By leveraging the resources of the moon and other celestial bodies, we can create a foundation for future missions to Mars and beyond, paving the way for the colonization of other worlds.

Moreover, future space exploration missions will be characterized by international collaboration and cooperation, bringing together nations from around the world to work towards a common goal. By pooling our resources, expertise, and knowledge, we can achieve feats of exploration and discovery that would be impossible for any single nation to accomplish alone.

In addition to human space exploration, future missions will also focus on robotic exploration of the solar system, sending spacecraft to explore distant planets, moons, and asteroids in search of signs of life and clues to the origins of the universe. By combining human and robotic exploration efforts, we can maximize our understanding of the cosmos and unlock the mysteries of the universe.

In conclusion, the legacy of Apollo 11 serves as a beacon of hope and inspiration for future generations as we look towards the future of space exploration. By building on the achievements of the past and embracing the challenges and opportunities of the future, we can continue to push the boundaries of exploration and discovery, unlocking the secrets of the cosmos and fulfilling humanity's destiny as a spacefaring species.

Chapter 14: Remembering Apollo 11

The Apollo 11 mission stands as one of humanity's greatest achievements, a testament to human ingenuity, courage, and determination. As the years have passed since that historic day in 1969, the memory of Apollo 11 and its significance have continued to captivate the imagination of people around the world. This chapter delves into the commemorations and tributes to the Apollo 11 mission over the years, the preservation of artifacts and sites related to the moon landing, and the enduring fascination with the achievement of landing a man on the moon.

Commemorations and Tributes to the Apollo 11 Mission:

Since the successful completion of the Apollo 11 mission, commemorations and tributes have been held around the world to honor the achievements of Neil Armstrong, Buzz Aldrin, Michael Collins, and the thousands of men and women who made the mission possible. From anniversary celebrations to museum exhibitions, these commemorations serve as a reminder of the significance of Apollo 11 in human history.

One of the most significant commemorations of the Apollo 11 mission is the annual celebration of the anniversary of the moon landing on July 20th. Each year, people around the world gather to mark the occasion with parades, ceremonies, and events honoring the bravery and courage of the Apollo 11 astronauts and celebrating the spirit of exploration and discovery.

In addition to anniversary celebrations, museums, science centers, and educational institutions around the world have curated exhibitions and displays showcasing artifacts, photographs, and memorabilia related to the Apollo 11 mission. These exhibitions offer visitors the opportunity to learn about the history and significance of the moon landing and to experience firsthand the wonder and excitement of space exploration.

Furthermore, the Apollo 11 mission has been commemorated in film, literature, music, and art, with countless works inspired by the courage and determination of the astronauts who made history. From documentaries and biographies to novels and paintings, these tributes pay homage to the legacy of Apollo 11 and its enduring impact on human culture and society.

The Preservation of Artifacts and Sites Related to the Moon Landing:

Preserving the artifacts and sites related to the Apollo 11 mission is essential for ensuring that future generations can learn about and appreciate the achievements of the past. From the lunar module Eagle to the footprints left by the astronauts on the moon's surface, these artifacts serve as tangible reminders of humanity's journey to the moon.

One of the most iconic artifacts related to the Apollo 11 mission is the lunar module Eagle, which carried Neil Armstrong and Buzz Aldrin to the surface of the moon. Although the lunar module itself remains on the lunar surface, replicas and models of Eagle can be found in museums and educational institutions around the world, allowing visitors to experience firsthand the spacecraft that made history.

In addition to the lunar module Eagle, other artifacts related to the Apollo 11 mission, including spacesuits, scientific instruments, and moon rocks, are carefully preserved and displayed in museums and science centers. These artifacts provide valuable insights into the technology and science behind the moon landing and serve as a testament to the dedication and ingenuity of the people who made it possible.

Moreover, the sites associated with the Apollo 11 mission, including the Kennedy Space Center in Florida, Mission Control in Houston, and the lunar landing site on the moon, are designated as historic landmarks and protected for future generations. Efforts are underway to preserve and maintain these sites, ensuring that they remain intact for future exploration and study.

The Enduring Fascination with the Achievement of Landing a Man on the Moon:

Despite the passage of time, the achievement of landing a man on the moon continues to captivate the imagination of people around the world. The moon landing of Apollo 11 represents a defining moment in human history—a testament to the power of human ingenuity and determination to overcome seemingly insurmountable challenges.

One of the reasons for the enduring fascination with the moon landing is its sheer audacity and ambition. In an age before smartphones, computers, and the internet, the idea of sending humans to the moon and returning them safely to Earth was nothing short of miraculous. The achievement of Apollo 11 inspired people around the world to dream big and reach for the stars.

Furthermore, the moon landing of Apollo 11 captured the imagination of people from all walks of life, transcending national boundaries and uniting people around the world in awe and wonder. The iconic images of Neil Armstrong taking his first steps on the lunar surface, Buzz Aldrin planting the American flag, and the Earth rising above the horizon served as a reminder of the fragility and beauty of our planet and inspired a renewed sense of wonder and curiosity about the cosmos.

Moreover, the moon landing of Apollo 11 represented a triumph of human cooperation and collaboration, as nations around the world came together to achieve a common goal. It served as a powerful symbol of what can be accomplished when we work together towards a shared vision of exploration and discovery.

In conclusion, the memory of Apollo 11 and its significance continue to resonate with people around the world, inspiring future generations to reach for the stars and explore the wonders of the cosmos. Through commemorations, preservation efforts, and ongoing exploration of the moon and beyond, the legacy of Apollo 11 will endure for generations to come, serving as a reminder of the power of human ingenuity, courage, and determination to achieve the impossible.

Chapter 15: Conclusion

The moon landing of Apollo 11 stands as a defining moment in human history—a testament to the power of human ingenuity, courage, and determination to explore the unknown and push the boundaries of exploration and discovery. As we reflect on the significance of the moon landing in the history of humanity, look ahead to the possibilities and challenges of future space exploration, and consider the enduring legacy of Apollo 11, we are reminded of the profound impact of this historic achievement on our collective consciousness and our vision for the future.

Reflecting on the Significance of the Moon Landing in the History of Humanity:

The moon landing of Apollo 11 marked the culmination of centuries of human curiosity and exploration, as people around the world looked up at the night sky and wondered what lay beyond the confines of Earth. It represented a triumph of human ingenuity and determination, as scientists, engineers, and astronauts worked tirelessly to overcome the challenges of space travel and achieve the seemingly impossible.

Moreover, the moon landing of Apollo 11 served as a symbol of hope and inspiration for people around the world, demonstrating what can be accomplished when we dare to dream big and reach for the stars. It reminded us of the boundless potential of the human spirit to overcome adversity and achieve greatness, inspiring future generations to pursue their dreams of exploration and discovery.

Looking Ahead to the Possibilities and Challenges of Future Space Exploration:

As we look ahead to the future of space exploration, we are faced with both incredible possibilities and daunting challenges. The exploration of space holds the promise of unlocking the mysteries of the cosmos, expanding our understanding of the universe, and discovering new worlds and civilizations beyond our own.

However, the challenges of space exploration are immense, requiring us to develop new technologies, overcome the harsh environment of space, and navigate the complexities of interplanetary travel. From the dangers of radiation and microgravity to the logistical challenges of long-duration missions, space exploration presents a host of obstacles that must be overcome if we are to realize our vision of exploring the cosmos.

Moreover, the quest for space exploration is not just a technical or scientific endeavor—it is also a moral and ethical one. As we venture out into the cosmos, we must confront questions of sustainability, equity, and responsibility, ensuring that our exploration of space benefits all of humanity and preserves the integrity of the universe for future generations.

The Enduring Legacy of Apollo 11 and its Importance in Inspiring Future Generations:

The legacy of Apollo 11 is one of inspiration, innovation, and discovery—a reminder of what can be accomplished when we work together towards a common goal. The achievements of Neil Armstrong, Buzz Aldrin, Michael Collins, and the thousands of men and women who made the mission possible continue to inspire and captivate people around the world, shaping our collective vision of the future.

Moreover, the legacy of Apollo 11 extends beyond the realm of space exploration, influencing every aspect of human culture and society.

From art and literature to science and technology, the moon landing of Apollo 11 has left an indelible mark on human history, inspiring new generations to pursue their dreams and reach for the stars.

As we reflect on the enduring legacy of Apollo 11, we are reminded of the power of human ingenuity, courage, and determination to overcome the greatest challenges and achieve the greatest dreams. The achievements of Apollo 11 serve as a beacon of hope and inspiration for future generations, reminding us that the human spirit knows no bounds when it comes to exploring the cosmos and unlocking the mysteries of the universe.

In conclusion, the moon landing of Apollo 11 represents a defining moment in human history—a testament to the power of human ingenuity, courage, and determination to explore the unknown and push the boundaries of exploration and discovery. As we look ahead to the future of space exploration, we carry with us the lessons and achievements of Apollo 11, and the knowledge that the human spirit knows no bounds when it comes to reaching for the stars.

Don't miss out!

Visit the website below and you can sign up to receive emails whenever Michael Johnson publishes a new book. There's no charge and no obligation.

https://books2read.com/r/B-A-OREFB-UDXAD

BOOKS 2 READ

Connecting independent readers to independent writers.

Did you love *The Moon Landing*? Then you should read *The Harlem Renaissance*[1] by Michael Johnson!

[2]

"Renaissance of the Harlem: Cultural Awakening in the African American Community" delves into the transformative era of the Harlem Renaissance, illuminating its origins, luminaries, and enduring legacy. From the influx of African Americans during the Great Migration to the emergence of literary giants like Langston Hughes and Zora Neale Hurston, this book explores the vibrant intersections of art, music, theater, and activism that defined Harlem in the early 20th century. With insightful analyses and profiles of key figures, it celebrates the cultural resurgence while acknowledging its complexities and challenges, offering a compelling narrative of empowerment and inspiration.

---

1. https://books2read.com/u/b6JjyZ

2. https://books2read.com/u/b6JjyZ

About the Author

Michael Johnson is a distinguished historian specializing in American history. With a degree in History from Harvard University, Johnson's work delves into pivotal moments, figures, and themes shaping the United States. He has authored numerous acclaimed books, offering insightful perspectives and engaging narratives. Johnson's commitment to meticulous scholarship and compelling storytelling has earned him widespread acclaim in the field. Passionate about sharing his expertise, he frequently engages in lectures and public events to foster a deeper appreciation for America's past.

www.ingramcontent.com/pod-product-compliance
Lightning Source LLC
Chambersburg PA
CBHW021138130726
47988CB00003B/1369